REAL WORLD HYPNOSIS
INSIDER TIPS FROM LEADING HYPNOTISTS

Edited by Steve Roh

Contributing Authors:
>Celeste Hackett
>
>Debbie Lane
>
>Wendy Merron
>
>Robert Dunscomb
>
>Marc Carlin
>
>Deborah Yaffee
>
>Garrett Buttel
>
>Tobin Slaven

www.RealWorldHypnosisBook.com

Published by:

Autarch Publishing

1735 Market St. Suite A-411

Philadelphia, PA 19103

fax: 866-224-7559

ISBN 978-0-6152-3904-0

TABLE OF CONTENTS

"The unorthodox and the orthodox give rise to each other, like a beginningless circle -- who could exhaust them?"

- Sun Tzu

INTRODUCTION

This book reflects the knowledge gathered by several leading hypnotists, based on real-world experience in addition to dedicated training over the course of many years.

There are many misconceptions about hypnosis that have resulted from Hollywood and TV images. Hypnosis is often sensationalized in an attempt to make it appear as a sort of bizarre mind-control that demonstrates the special powers of the hypnotist.

The fact is, "getting hypnotized" is a remarkably simple and natural process. With basic training and the confidence that comes with practice, it is almost a trivial exercise to be able to coach someone into that natural state of mind. But the real test of any professional hypnotist is what they can do once they get a person into that state--- especially if they can help an individual achieve a desired change.

The contributors to this book are successful practitioners with years of experience. Their desire to use their skills and talents to help others shines through. This book is an effort to help spread the good word about hypnosis by sharing their practical advice and insight.

Steve Roh

Consulting Hypnotist and Editor

Philadelphia, PA

July 2008

CHAPTER 1

Ten Tips for Starting a Hypnosis Practice on a Budget

By Celeste Hackett, CH CPHI

> *"It is great wealth to a soul to live frugally with a contented mind."*
>
> Lucretius

For years I wanted to own my own business, but didn't think I had what it takes. I thought that people who started a company must have something everyone else doesn't have, some kind of special smart gene or something. What I'd like to show you in this chapter, is that no special smart gene is required to start a hypnosis practice that works. You just need to know a few insider tips. And you do have to have some good sense about money because if you don't, you'll fail.

Being able to budget, putting money aside to save up for things, saying no to something you know you don't need right now, even when you have a strong desire for it, shopping around for the best prices, and knowing what you are willing to lose are some of the things common to those with good money sense. If you don't have any idea what I am talking about you are not alone. This is why most Americans live paycheck to paycheck and credit card bill to credit card bill. This perfectly illustrates tip number one.

Tip number one: Get control of your personal spending first. It's common knowledge among business experts that problems and successes trickle down from the top in a business. A person who is a good communicator is going to value good communicators and hire those who know how to positively motivate employees. Alternatively, a boss who rules with an iron fist is going to model that behavior and his mid-management won't be very nice to work for. Why is that? It's because people, to a very large degree, bring their knowledge, expertise and mental and emotional make-up into their work lives. In the same way, your business will be an extension of your strengths and weaknesses be it management style, communication or checks and balances.

So what do you do if your personal Finances are a mess? Relax. There is plenty of hope. Loads of people have overcome this problem and you can too. I recommend doing a Google search on such search terms as: "Frugal living", "living on a budget" and "getting out of debt". There are loads of websites, message boards and books on the subject that can help you. Also go to www.amazon.com and do a search there on: Becoming debt-free.

Two of my favorite books are: The Tightwad Gazette by Amy Dacyczyn (an older book full of motivation to cut back on spending) and The Total Money Makeover by Dave Ramsey. Also, don't forget radio shows that support and encourage you while you are learning how to stay within a budget and pay off debt. Dave Ramsey has a radio show you can listen to on-line and it's so inspiring you'll be hypnotized into getting your money under your control!

Tip number two: Make a list of what you *need* - to do your business effectively and shop around for the best prices. That sounds simple enough. Doesn't it? But something happens to people when they get the "I'm going to start my own practice" fever. Their emotions become involved. They do emotional spending. Some spend on expensive things to feel like they are successful when they aren't yet. Some overspend to look successful to others in an attempt to reduce their fear of being seen as not being good enough. Some are just so overwhelmed by the process of starting a new business that they'll overspend to make it easier and faster getting started.

The remedy for this is, again, just relax. Allow yourself *time* to think about what you need and shop around. Setting up a business can take time, so make the time. Otherwise you'll end up starting out on the wrong foot with expensive stuff and you'll be in major debt before you even get your first client. As far as being worried about how you'll be perceived, as long as you have a good enough place and good enough things in it, you'll be just fine.

When I first began, I started out of my apartment in Dallas. The complex where we lived was rather old, was 3 flights upstairs and right next to a regularly over-flowing dumpster. I didn't think anyone would come, but I was so wrong! When they did come I began to formulate all sorts of ideas for overcoming any objections they might have about me working out of an apartment. It didn't take me long at all to realize that they didn't care about *where* I worked or what kind of chair I was sitting in. All they had on their minds, and all they wanted to know was, could I help them overcome their pain. They were so focused on their problem that my being in an apartment hardly seemed to register.

Tip number three: Make sure you've got good training to start with. Good training is your foundation and you don't want to scrimp on it. That being said, excellent training is very affordable. You'll be really excited about how affordable it is when compared to a university degree program that prepares you for a career.

For instance, my niece will be starting an associate degree program (2 years long) in nursing at Louisiana State University in Alexandria this upcoming fall. The program is completed in 5 semesters each costing $2,794.25. That comes to $13,971.00 for a two year program! Add to this the cost of books, travel and although she won't pay for lodging, some students will. Very good hypnosis training, at the time of this writing, can be gotten for between $1500-2500.00 in total and it only takes about 10 days!

When you look for good training be sure and get that which teaches you both basic and advanced techniques - Rapid and instant inductions, depth testing, convincers, age regression, forgiveness methods for self and others and techniques for dealing with secondary gain. You want to learn real hypnosis that really works not relaxation masquerading as hypnosis.

Also, make sure the program offers you plenty of time to practice what you learn in class and that you get on-going support, training and/or supervision that is cheap or free because you'll need it. Actually *doing* the sessions is where you will really get your education, so you'll need guidance and encouragement from time to time.

Don't skip over this tip because, I've known a lot of hypnotists who started out with poor training and just didn't make it. The ones that did make it either had to get more training or they began doing other things like EFT or energy work. I have to wonder if it is because they never got to see the big bang of hypnosis phenomena and change in clients consistently, or even at all.

Tip number four: Get some business training. What does this mean? Learn record keeping, how to book appointments on the phone, how to collect your fee, how to market your practice, How to manage your income and expenses, and how to pay taxes. You'll learn some of this in your hypnosis training program, but I have to recommend a product that has paid off for me exponentially: Maureen Banyan's business pack. Because of her, I simply make more money. Why? Because, among other things, I now take credit cards and I book 5 session packages instead of one session at a time. You can go to www.hypnosiscenter.com to find out more about Maureen Banyan's business training. It's only fifty dollars!

Tip number five: Sign up with a credit card company and ask for their dial pay service. Dial pay is the cheapest way to take credit cards that I know of.   You don't have to have a machine. Your clients give you their credit card number, expiration date, street address and zip code. You dial an 800#, and follow several prompts. They ask for: Your personal code, if you are going to charge a client's card or credit them, their credit card number, expiration date, street address, zip code, and the amount of the transaction. Then, they approve the sell right there on the phone. One thing I love about taking credit cards is, if you get a good company, they'll put the funds in your account within 24 hours.

Tip number six: Consider working from home. I do and I love it! My utilities and office rent are free! Rent may be the biggest expense you'll have. I can use my personal computer, telephone, fax and desk that I already own, and I get a tax write off for my home office. Also, I don't have a commute so I am in my robe and fuzzy slippers until right before my first client comes in at 9am! It's great!

If you do decide to work from home please know you are taking a risk in personal safety. I make sure my husband is here when I see male clients and I'm planning to get a personal panic button that alerts the police in the event of an emergency. Bad things do happen to good people, but they happen in big office buildings too.

To learn more ways to be safe while working at home consider a personal alarm: http://realestatesafety.com/ and let other's know your work day schedule. If possible have someone home with you. Don't use a sexy photo of yourself in advertising. Have mace nearby your door and hypno-chair. Use your intuition about people. Don't book anyone you aren't sure about. To learn more Google: Personal safety tips. Also check out my early articles at www at www.hypnosiscenter.com where I offer more on the safety aspects of working from home.

Tip number seven: Second best idea for low rent? Subletting. Yes, you can sublet from another office. After working in my apartment, I worked in a acupuncturist's office for a little while. He had a very nice set up with a receptionist and a waiting room in a beautiful medical building. I paid only $300 per month and it was fun having the company of another working professional around too.

Tip number eight: Use the Internet to advertise. Mostly, internet advertising and marketing are cheap. First, get a website that looks good. A great website is worth the money. I spent about $1000.00 on mine, but you can get them cheaper. Also, consider listing your services on Craig's list and boards like it. Phone directories on-line can be good. Some are free but most are cheap such as (2006 prices below):

-Magic yellow ($63 per month)

-Smart pages ($10 per month)

-Dallas Yellow pages ($35 per month)

You can also create a "Meet up" Group at www.meetup.com. Meetup is the world's largest network of self-organized clubs and community groups. These groups help people meet others in their area who share their interests and gives them a way to learn, teach and share things.

Other ways to advertise on-line cheap or free are to buy space on a website that is highly ranked and has high traffic for people interested in hypnosis, trade links with other websites that are complimentary and that have high SEO and put your business slogan in your signature on your email. These can be inexpensive ways of getting the word out about your business.

Tip number nine: Get out and meet people. Pass out flyers and cards. Tell everyone what you do. Post flyers and give free talks about hypnosis. Mail or drop off your information to Doctors, massage therapists, chiropractors, acupuncturists, dentists, therapists and health clubs. Your energy will come back to you in clients. Some things will work better than others, so be patient while you are learning how to network and market like this.

Tip number ten: Ask your clients for referrals. Make sure you let them know you are taking on new clients. Ask them, who do you know who needs my help? Give them cards each time they come in even if you already have. You want to keep the idea that you are looking for referrals top of mind with them. I jokingly tell my clients, "I know you already have some of my cards, that's okay, here's some more! Just put them in the break room at work or in the bathroom at the library or drop them accidentally on the floor in the foyer of your office building."

Also, don't forget to put up a sign that says you are accepting referrals. Mine is in the bathroom and says, "Please tell a friend about our services." I also leave a few cards on the counter in there. Don't forget when you get a referral, to follow up with a thank you and more cards.

You may come up with some other keys of your own that work. If you do, don't' forget to pass them on. I know I'd love to hear about them. Oh, that leads to a bonus tip: Help out your fellow hypnotist every once in a while with support, encouragement and information. One of the secret laws of success in the universe is when you help others get the success they want; you'll get the success what you want too.

~~~

About Celeste Hackett, CH CPHI

Dallas, TX

Celeste Hackett became a hypnotist after a long and rewarding career as a major market Radio announcer. She sees about 13- 20 clients a week in Dallas, Texas, encountering a wide range of issues where mostly she uses 5-PATH and other advanced methodologies.

Celeste Hackett has been featured on the Kidd Kraddick Radio Show, and in Dallas Child magazine. She supports new hypnotists in various ways such as my quarterly articles at www.banyanhypnosiscenter.com.

In addition, Celeste is currently working on starting a state-licensed hypnosis school, and co-hosts a weekly Web-TV Show with Calvin Banyan called "Cal Banyan's Hypnosis Etc with Celeste Hackett." You can access their show at www.calbanyan.com.

You can also contact Celeste at Celestehackett@yahoo.com or 972-673-0110 and view her website at www.familyfirsthypnosis.com.

CHAPTER 2

Silencing Hiccups

By Debbie Lane

> *"Thought is the sculptor who can create the person you want to be."*
> Henry David Thoreau

My name is Debbie Lane, certified Hiccupnotist. Since February 28, 2007, that is how I often introduce myself. My story started one morning as I was going through my morning routine of quiet contemplation and reading the paper before my business day begins. On this particular day, I read an article about a 15 year old girl who was suffering from a case of non stop hiccups. According to the article, the hiccups began in her science class for no apparent reason. They were loud, so loud as to be disruptive to the class. The young lady with the hiccups was sent to the clinic and then sent home. The hiccups continued. She tried all the usual cures. Nothing worked. Eventually, out of desperation, her mother appealed to the media.

A reporter met this young woman and her mother and wrote about her plight in the newspaper, The St. Petersburg Times and I was drawn to the article. It was buried deep within the paper, almost as an after thought the first time it ran. I felt so bad for this young girl. I am the mother of 2 sons, one who was the same age and grade as she was.

My son has had tremendous health challenges as well. Two years prior to this he had life altering surgeries that meant he was now able to walk up a flight of stairs at school without having to stop and rest. Now, he was healthy and happy. I wanted this girl to have the same.

So, I emailed the reporter. I told her I was touched and that I am a hypnotist. I never promised a cure, just offered help, if it was wanted. The reporter wrote back, stating she had forwarded my note and she thought that was so nice.

The story was picked up by other media outlets. It became national, then international news. The young girl tried chiropractic, acupuncture, gastroenterology, regular MD's and a cup claiming to cure hiccups. When her mother was told that the only solution was invasive and expensive surgery, she decided to call me.

I will never forget that phone call. I was in a local breakfast restaurant waiting for a gal from my networking group to show up. She never showed. As I was about to leave, my cell phone rang, it was the mom. She wanted to know if I was still willing to work with her daughter. We set up an appointment for two days later at 4:00.

When the Hiccup Chick (as the media lovingly labeled her) and her mother and her best friend arrived, the hiccups were so loud, the receptionist took her to a conference room at the far end of the office building to wait.

Before the session, I sat and journaled for 15 minutes. I had done a personal hypnosis session before bed the previous two nights. I had dreamt about the session and how it would go. I repeated with another session this particular morning and journaled again. So, here I sat, asking for wisdom, for guidance, for protocol, for something, for anything! "Just please let me help her", I wrote. I wrote that over and over. Then the words appeared on my page, "Listen to the quiet, notice the stillness; that is where your answers lie." What? She was so loud people were laughing in the hallways about the noise from the other end of the offices. What stillness?

"In stillness her fears appear and she disappears", the paper said. This confused me. But, it was time for the appointment. After all, I hadn't promised a cure. I said a quick prayer. One I often say before any session.

"God, this is about my client, not about me. Release my ego so that I can be used to guide the client without interfering."

I gulped and walked the longest walk of my career. This young lady was sweet and typical of any 15 year old girl. She and her friend made jokes and giggled. Mom seemed tired. She agreed to my working with her daughter alone, I agreed to record the entire session for them. Mom and the friend went out for a snack together.

The hiccups slowed down the more I listened to her, really listened as she spoke about herself, her school, and her dreams. The hiccups that had kept her in an uproar, barely sleeping for 38 days seemed to become quieter.

I learned about her home life and with all that was going on; to her it seemed she got lost in the confusion. Now, she had been gifted with a new computer from a local retailer so she could keep up with her school work and provided with a private homebound tutor by the school system. A local theater had set up a private showing of a movie she wanted to see for her and 30 friends! She was interviewed on a local radio show, she was becoming a media darling, yet all she said she wanted was to "be normal".

I began with some relaxation with her. All of this had taken a toll on her and she was exhausted. This seemed to be a welcome relief. These techniques were ones she could use afterwards on her own. Next, we regressed her to a time prior to the hiccups. During this time, the hiccups disappeared. We were able to revisit the day they began and allow her to recall how she felt prior to the hiccups. We followed this by determining what part of her wanted her to keep the hiccups, what the motive was. She felt fear, fear for her health, and fear her body would do something more dramatic health wise to keep her validated.

We validated her importance to her family, her friends, herself. We thanked the fear for allowing us to be aware of how important she is and we released fear.

I brought her back up and we discussed what she had just experienced. The hiccups returned, softly this time and less frequently. Nothing violent, just enough to let us know there was more work to be done.

So, again, she entered a state of relaxation. She went deeper this time; she looked like an angel in the chair across the room from me. The way a mother sees their 2 year old when sleeping after a day of terrorizing.

I allowed her to rest. Then, we began to work with blue lights to heal her throat charka. This young woman had not felt heard in a house with siblings and stepsiblings, an aunt and uncle, disabled stepfather and over worked mother!

As is above, is below. So, we balanced her solar plexus as well. To accomplish this, we created a sense of self empowerment without the hiccups. Finally, I gave direct suggestions to be able to bring this relaxed state and newfound communication forward with her into her daily living. We also gave her an anchor for future use. (A "hypnotic anchor" is any stimulus that triggers a consistent psychological state or more simply stated, a hypnotic anchor is an association to any life memory.)

When we were complete, she opened her eyes, hiccup free, with tears streaming down her face. "Oh my God, you don't know how much I love you" she spoke. It was 6:01p.m. We both cried tears of joy.

The news of the stopping of the hiccups received international attention. After much press, the phone calls began to pour in; so many people with so many needs, from all over the country. The son of a gentleman who had been hiccupping for 4 years contacted me. He was 72 years old; his son (a New York City cop) was worried about the toll it was taking on him. So, we agreed to meet. He flew down; he and his wife frequently visit my area of Florida. Again, I prepared with a self hypnosis session and journaling. "Please, help me help this man. Please, guide me, help me help this man." This time the paper said, "Peace, be still."

The first day we met, we chatted about his hiccups. They were insistent bouts of hiccupping when they came upon him. He felt constant pain and fatigue as a result. We discussed what he felt when they were about to begin.

Prior to his coming in for the visit, I had sent him a relaxation audio I had developed for him, based on a phone conversation. He listened to it daily for 2 weeks. He felt it was already helping. One of the issues that came up for him was that he no longer felt useful. He had once been the Grand Marshall of a major parade in NYC! He had run the NYC transit system and now felt less vital. I recognized a common theme. He was a devout Irish Catholic. So, I asked him who his favorite figure was in religious history. He immediately shared the story of Padre Pio.

During our first session, we again regressed to prior to the first bout of hiccups and noticed what changes were occurring in his life at that time. He addressed his feelings about them, and validated him as useful without defining himself through his work. I reminded him of Padre Pio. He was deep in trance; he seemed to be busy without speaking a word, so I became silent and allowed whatever was happening to continue. When it was complete, he emerged and smiled. He felt calm, relaxed and ready to travel!

We met two more times prior to his leaving town. Each of those meeting were focused on specific questions he had, balancing with the blue lights and creating anchors for him related to situations where hiccups had been an issue in the past.

I had a woman call me who had been burping for 2 years solid. Can you imagine? 38 burps, every 15 minutes she reported. It was affecting her work and her social life, especially her marriage. We had amazing results first session. It turned out, we discovered, when we regressed her to prior to the burping that the company she was employed by had been sold and that her daughter and she had issues arise, all about the time the burping began. The sale of the company had created a big shift in her role at work, she felt for the worse. Her daughter, an adult, was angry and blaming mom for everything she possibly could. No explanations or apologies were accepted, they fell on deaf ears. Once again, here was someone who felt the need to be heard and validated. Other situations in her personal and work life were all contributing to a belief that she was not feeling heard or validated. Therefore, we worked on her personal validation.

After the initial session, she left my office burp free. She listened to the audio I provided for her and did 3 follow up sessions. She still calls on occasion for other issues and boosters.

I have been referred to in a humorous fashion as the "Personal Emissions Expert". Truth be told, what I do best is listen. When a client feels heard, they find out themselves, just what the cause of a problem is. Our bodies reflect our thoughts and belief. Our bodies are telling us what is out of balance, it is simply learning to listen that can make the difference. I do hypnotic journaling. I write to my higher wisdom before many of my sessions about a given situation and ask for guidance. While a new client is filling out paperwork and listening to an audio I have prepared for first visits, I am busy journaling. With repeat clients, I schedule time between clients to be able to focus on them and journal.

I write out the question, my concerns and whatever flows. I write quickly and with intent. It is not going to be read by anyone else, often I don't even read it again, I trash it. But, by writing faster than my inner critic can speak, I am able to open up to answers and information. The answers flow through my hand onto the paper. This is particularly helpful if I first take a hypnosis break. My friend and author of <u>Writing Down Your Soul</u>, Janet Conner did extensive research on this and found out that the brain goes into a theta state when doing this type of writing, it can also go into mystical theta. The combination of the two, hypnosis and soul writing creates a quick entry into mystical theta.

I always ask that my ego is taken out of the equation. Hopefully, we (hypnotherapists) all do. For me it is an important part of the process to specifically request this in a prayer format.

Not everyone has hiccups or burps on a continual basis. We *all* have signals from our bodies, however, when attention is lacking in one area of our lives or another. It is important that you pay attention to your body, listen before the signals go from a whisper to the sirens of the emergency vehicle taking you to the hospital or worse.

- Take two minutes, twice a day to become completely quiet. Once you are relaxed and still, scan your body for any areas of discomfort and notice where that is. Breathe into that area and allow comfort to begin. Ask your higher wisdom what this is trying to tell you.
- Notice what your first thoughts are. If you are still, they may drift towards an issue that has been bothering you. If you are resistant to change, the thoughts may be more about what is on your <u>To Do</u> list.
- Continue bringing your thoughts back to what the discomfort represents to you. (Just as the hiccups were related to not feeling heard.) Then begin to imagine yourself if that need was being met. (Imagine your loved ones or work mates, peers etc. listening to your concerns and perhaps nodding as they listened.)

- Create a positive statement that reflects the need. (I am heard and appreciated now.) Repeat that statement silently to yourself as you imagine being heard and appreciated.

- Finally, look in the mirror and repeat your affirmation. Look into your eyes as you state the affirmation. If this is difficult, repeat it consistently through out the day. I tell many of my clients to repeat affirmations every time they first get into their car to drive somewhere. The rearview mirror is the perfect size for eye contact.

~~~

About Debbie Lane, C.Ht.

There is a reason that Debbie Lane C.Ht. is the top hypnotherapist in Tampa Bay. She is the International Hypnotist of the Year 2007 and is well known for her work with the Hiccup Girl as well as other high profile and complex cases. Lane runs a thriving practice in Palm Harbor, Florida.

Call Debbie at: (727) 781-8483 or email her at wisdomhypnosis@yahoo.com.

Visit www.WisdomHypnosis.com for stories, videos, testimonials, and Debbie's blog. Debbie offers a free stress reduction audio at her website for your listening pleasure.

CHAPTER 3

Weight Loss

By Wendy Merron

> *"Eating diet food is about as satisfying as watching an action film of a snail race."*
>
> - Wendy Merron

My personal opinion is that packaged diet foods are usually both tasteless and unsatisfying. When low fat foods first appeared on grocery shelves, I remember purchasing a box of low-fat chocolate cookies. Like many others, I was enthralled that they were low in fat. No fat – No guilt!. The idea of munching down as many as I wanted was so appealing! So I ate one. And another. And another. And another. Why did I eat so many? The cookies were bland and dull. They were not appealing at all. The truth is I kept eating them because I was hoping that eventually they would taste satisfying and I would enjoy them.

If you are thinking about going on a diet, you are doomed to fail. Why? Because diet foods taste like twice-baked sweat socks? No. You are doomed to fail because most diets require deprivation, and depriving ourselves NEVER WORKS to lose weight.

"No", you are thinking, "This can't be true. I have a friend who went on a diet and lost weight." We all have friends who have lost weight. And some have kept it off. Perhaps you have lost weight too. But have you kept it off for more than a year? Or did you find yourself slowing adding those extra pounds right back on over the next few months?

If you've lost weight only to find yourself regaining those pounds (and sometimes more), then why do it all over again? There's only one reason: You learned from the past, and you plan to do things differently. You know that eating less and moving more is simply NOT ENOUGH to ensure success, or you wouldn't be reading this.

The SECRET THIRD COMPONENT to success is to use the power of your mind to take the struggle out of losing weight.

In this chapter you will learn:

- Why diets don't work
- How to tell if you have Emotional Eating Problems
- How to Eliminate Emotional Eating
- Why eliminating foods will cause you to GAIN weight
- How to dine out and still lose weight
- What you need to do EVERY DAY for 5 minutes to reach and MAINTAIN your goals.

Why don't diets work? Because most diets consist of a way to eat in which you are depriving yourself of specific foods. Weight Watchers, by-the-way, is not considered a diet in my opinion. It is well defined food related program designed to help you learn to make lifelong healthy food choices. Unfortunately, like other food related programs, Weight Watchers does not teach you how to THINK about yourself and food.

The way we think, imagine, and feel about ourselves and food is directly related to how easy it is to lose weight and maintain our weight.

When I decided that I was finally going to lose weight once and for all, I came to the conclusion that eliminating white flour and sugar from my diet was the way to go. I wanted to learn how to make healthy choices and I know that most processed foods and baked goods contain these ingredients. And because white flour and sugar have little or no nutritional value I figured these were the best to eliminate.

Have you ever gone on a diet and eliminated specific foods that you enjoy?

It's no fun. And it's really hard to stick to it. After a week or so, I found myself feeling really deprived. Even worse, I found myself thinking about cookies, ice cream and cake every day. The more I deprived myself, the more I thought about these foods. (Just for the record, these are the foods that contributed in a big way to the 173 pounds I was carrying on my 5 foot 1 inch frame.)

A few weeks later, after using more will-power than I knew I had, I came to the conclusion that my mind was acting like a spoiled two year old. The more I said "NO!" to sweets - the more my mind WANTED sweets. I was struggling with wanting every day! To say I was miserable was an understatement.

One day I decided to end the struggle. At that time I knew that I was finally in total control of everything I ate. I knew that I could have a dish of ice cream and still stick to my diet. My confidence and will-power were strong. I had lost 8 pounds and was on my way to a new me. So I sat down and had a small dish of chocolate marshmallow ice cream. It was wonderful. Cold, smooth, sweet and creamy, I loved that delightful feeling as it melted on my tongue. After I finished the ice cream, I put my dish in the dishwasher and left the kitchen.

As I continued throughout the evening I couldn't stop thinking about how good that ice cream tasted. Should I have just a little bit more? I've lost 8 pounds, so I can afford to have a little bit more. Maybe I'll take just another small serving. I took the ice cream container out of the freezer and put another serving in a new bowl and sat down to watch TV. Let's fast forward to the end of the evening. It may not be a surprise to many of you that I single-handedly finished that entire container of chocolate marshmallow ice cream.

Was I in total control? Heck no. I couldn't seem to stop myself. Did I enjoy it? It tasted wonderful at the time. But when I was finished I felt awful. Hugely upset with myself that I had consumed a whole gallon of ice cream in one evening. I felt as if I had just undone 2 weeks of dieting in one sitting. I was mad at myself for allowing myself to eat so much ice cream. Did I gain weight? I wish I could say "No, I didn't gain any weight," but this wasn't a fantasy. It was real life. And it was a real big gallon of high fat, high calorie chocolate marshmallow ice cream.

The next day I decided that dieting and eliminating foods I enjoyed was the wrong way to approach eating. It just didn't work. To be honest, I was never successful with this approach. It was then that I decided that the only way for me to let go of excess pounds was to create a new way of eating that works for ME. Following someone else's version of what's right and wrong, or good and bad wasn't working.

At that moment I decided to allow myself to have something sweet every day. I decided that it was up to me to choose how many calories of chocolate, cookies, cake, etc., that I would allow myself.. I even decided that I could CHANGE the number of calories that I chose to consume. What fun! I get to eat chocolate! Cookies! Cake! Ice Cream! Woo Hoo!

What happened next wasn't surprising. I found myself beginning to LOOK FORWARD to choosing something sweet to eat every day. For the next few days, I couldn't wait to consume anything that I wanted. (Within my personal calorie limit, of course.) Something had shifted inside of me. Eating this way was FUN!

A few weeks later as I was describing my new way of eating to a friend, she asked me "What kind of special chocolaty sweet treat did you eat today?" I stopped to think. I hadn't had anything sweet that day. I hadn't eaten anything sweet the day before, either. Or the day before that. I couldn't believe the words that came out of my mouth, "I haven't had chocolate for about a week, I said. "In fact, I rarely think about it the way I used to. Once I ALLOWED myself to eat some every day I no longer felt deprived, and no longer thought about chocolate."

That day I came up with these personal rules:

Rule # 1. Depriving myself feels bad and doesn't work.

Rule # 2. Eliminating my favorite foods causes me to eat too much and

gain weight.

Let's talk about Emotional Hunger and Physical Hunger. The concept of Emotional Hunger sounds complicated and difficult to describe. The truth is that it is simple. Here's how to tell the difference between physical and emotional hunger:

Physical hunger is a feeling that begins in your stomach. It starts with a little feeling and if it's not attended to (i.e. fed) it continues to grow and grow. Some find that they notice a gnawing or even growling feeling in their stomach. It's a real feeling. It's a feeling that most Americans today have little experience with because food is plentiful and easily accessible. In the past (years and years past) we tended to eat when we received the signal that our stomach was experiencing hunger. Now we tend to eat when our minds tell us we want something, rather than wait for that feeling to appear in our stomachs.

Emotional hunger is quite different. And quite easy to distinguish from physical hunger. Emotional hunger comes on very quickly. It often appears as a thought such as "Oooooh….I think a taste of that would be perfect right now." "I think I'll have a second helping." "I'd better eat now because I don't know when I'm going to have dinner." It often appears as a reflex, showing up whenever we walk through the kitchen and grab something to eat as we head to the next room.

What can you do with this new knowledge? You can begin to use it to learn more about yourself, your feelings, and your body. Connecting with your feelings, emotions and desires is a great start to improving your life. For me it was my first foray into experiencing the "Mind, Body, Spirit" connection.

Here's what you can do beginning today:

Every time you bring something to your mouth check in with your body. Ask yourself "Am I experiencing that hungry feeling in my stomach?"

If you are, then notice if you are making a good choice for yourself. If you are not hungry, you can examine what you are feeling. This takes practice, so don't feel discouraged if you can't figure it out all the time. And if you are not hungry, WALK AWAY from the food. Do not look back! Find other ways to distract yourself from food at that exact moment.

Rule # 3. Eliminating Emotional eating is a huge component to Losing Weight

Rule # 4. Find new ways to distract yourself from food

Now that you know it's not a good idea to eat when you aren't feeling hunger, what do you do when you are in a restaurant with friends? Not eat? Decide not to go if you aren't hungry? Give up dining out while you are letting go of excess weight? Of course not! It's time to develop some new coping mechanisms so you can continue to enjoy your social life and spend time with friends and family.

Below are a few tips that will help you when you dine out:

- Eat more slowly so that you feel fuller faster.
- Be the last one to begin eating. You'll end up with food on your plate while others have scarfed down their entire meal.
- Put half of your food in a take out container BEFORE you begin to eat
- Take a sip of water between every bite to slow yourself down.
- If you are counting calories, only eat foods when you know the calories count.
- Make a game of putting your utensils down frequently

By this time you are probably wondering what hypnosis has to do with any of these suggestions for losing weight. There are three key components to successful Weight Loss:

1. Eat less. (You already knew this)
2. Move more. (Not a surprise) and
3. Take the Struggle out of Weight Loss with Hypnosis and the Emotional Freedom Technique (EFT)

If you consistently find that you lose weight just to gain it back later on, then you know that eating less and moving more just isn't enough. If you keep on doing what you are doing, you'll continue to get the same results. I promise.

If this sounds like you, it's time for you to add the all important Third Component (#3 above) to your life. One of the major concepts that I teach my clients is that our imagination is MUCH MORE POWERFUL than our personal will power.

Think about this. Which of the following would you rather experience every day?

1. Thinking about your body, heavy with excess weight, and imagining yourself struggling every day with your diet?

     Or

2. Imagining yourself as you want to be…trim, healthy, smiling, happy and in total control of everything you eat?

Take a moment and think about a time you've achieved success in your life. Maybe you learned something new, did something great at work, or successfully accomplished a task. Think back to this time of success. When you were in the process of achieving this success, what did you focus on? What did you think about? What kinds of images and thoughts went through your mind? Did you think about failing miserably, or did you imagine your success?

If you imagined your success, you know instinctively that focusing on what you DESIRED was one of the key components to your success. I personally take time to do this every day. I imagine myself the way I want to be. Some days it's only for a minute, right before I go to sleep. Some days I think about it a few times a day.

When I create my hypnosis CD's, help clients, and hold workshops for Weight Loss, Public Speaking and Smoking Cessation, I emphasize this concept frequently.

I can assure you that focusing on what you DESIRE will ALWAYS get you where you want to be. In my case, I've kept those 35 pounds off for over a year now. And for the first time in my life the journey has been without struggle.

Hypnosis and EFT have changed my life. They can change your life too.

~~~

About Wendy Merron

Wendy Merron is a Motivational Speaker & Trainer specializing in Weight Loss and Public Speaking. She is the President of the National Guild of Hypnotists (NGH) Greater Philadelphia Chapter, and an NGH Certified Hypnosis Instructor. Wendy Merron Goldenthal has been featured in numerous periodicals including Better Homes and Gardens, Main Line Today Magazine, the Suburban & Wayne Times, and Main Line Life. In addition she has presented at Philadelphia College of Osteopathic Medicine, Bryn Mawr Hospital, West Chester University, and the National Guild of Hypnotists Annual Conference.

To learn more about how you can lose weight permanently with Hypnosis and EFT, please contact Wendy at wgoldenthal@gmail.com or visit her site http://www.WendyMerron.com . (If you mention this book she will send you a free Hypnosis MP3 for Relaxation.)

CHAPTER 4

Hypnosis Can Help You Quit Smoking!

By Robert M Dunscomb, BCH

"Tobacco is a filthy weed,
that from the devil does proceed,

It drains your purse, it burns your clothes
and makes a chimney of your nose."

-Benjamin Waterhouse

"For thy sake Tobacco, I
would do anything but die."

-Charles Lamb

Why is it so difficult to stop smoking? When distinguished 19th Century essayist Charles Lamb was told by his "sour physician" that he must quit smoking, he wrote to a friend: "Surely there must be some other world in which this unconquerable purpose shall be realized".

Lamb's doctor gave him really good reasons to quit, but he could not force him to do so. Only Lamb himself could do that. If you're a smoker with good reasons to quit, the same applies to you. But, you're in luck -- you can get help that was not available to Lamb, in the form of hypnosis.

First, understand that no hypnotist can *make* you stop smoking. The only person who can make you stop smoking is the person who made you start... Think now... Who was that character anyway?

Yes by golly, you are right, it was *you*!

To make a long story short, here's why it can be so hard to quit. You had reasons to start, and maybe they seemed like pretty good reasons at the time. Perhaps you wanted to rebel against your parent's authority, perhaps you wanted to show that you really belonged to a group of friends who smoked, perhaps you just thought it was cool. Whatever those reasons were, are they still good enough? Good enough to keep you from stopping? Until you stop smoking, you are burning up your dollars and you are burning up your lungs. In a very real sense, you are burning up your life.

So now, you have very good reasons to stop smoking. You know quite well that it would be good for your health, good for your wallet and good for your quality of life to stop smoking...

You *know* that! Or... do you really?

The part of you that we call the *conscious mind* does indeed know all that. But there's another part of you that does not really understand and in fact doesn't even care about any of that. The part we call the *subconscious mind* still thinks that the reasons you started to smoke are good ones. It does not want you to stop smoking. And it's a fact that when there is a conflict between the conscious and the subconscious minds, the subconscious almost always wins.

So your subconscious mind has the *wrong ideas* about smoking. Old, outdated, obsolete ideas that should be left back there, years ago in the past, where they originated.

How do we let your subconscious mind know all that, so it can change?
How do we let your subconscious mind know all that, so *You* can change?

How do we help your subconscious mind understand, so that you can stop smoking easily and quickly?

Here's how: As you may know, professional hypnosis is a process of communicating with and educating the subconscious mind for the purpose of making positive changes in one's life. When you are ready to stop smoking, hypnosis can help you quit!

That's the short part of "the long and short of it". What follows is the "long" part, information about the cigarette habit that may help you make up your mind to quit.

The Smoking Habit:

People sometimes refer to smoking as if it were only an addiction to nicotine, like an addiction to cocaine or heroin. Nicotine raises your blood sugar, constricts your blood vessels and raises your blood pressure. When you started to smoke you became accustomed to those physical effects, which are numerous (and on the whole destructive). When you stop smoking you may experience some discomfort because those effects, which you are used to, are no longer there. Any such discomfort usually disappears within 72 hours, the approximate length of time needed to purge traces of nicotine from your body. These physiological effects are an important part of the smoking experience, but there is much more to the smoking habit than just the effects of nicotine.

Nicotine is not the end of the story. If it were, people could stop smoking by transferring their supposed drug addiction to other sources of nicotine, such as nicotine patches or chewing gums. While still suffering the negative effects of that poisonous drug, at least they would not be inhaling carcinogenic tars and scores or hundreds of other chemical toxins into their mouths, throats and lungs.

Now, I admit I don't hear about everything that goes on in and around Planet Earth, but I've yet to hear of a single case where a person has done this; that is, replaced an addiction to cigarettes with an addiction to nicotine gum or patches. It may have happened and no one has told me about it, but in any case, I certainly would not recommend it.

The reason that this doesn't happen is simple. Smoking is a *bad habit*, not unlike biting your fingernails - except a *lot* more dangerous and expensive! The habit becomes part of our subconscious programming. We are programmed to reach for and light up a cigarette at certain times when we receive various cues.

Do you identify with any of these cues?

You settle in behind the wheel of your car, click your seat belt and . . .

You've just finished a good meal and . . .

You pick up the phone and . . .

You pour yourself a cup of coffee and . . .

You meet friends for drink, and before you take your second sip . . .

You reach for a cigarette.

Professional hypnosis is way to help you reprogram these subconscious cues, eliminate them, and give you back control of your life.

Stop Smoking and Get Rich?

If you are a smoker, the habit not only costs you money, it could be costing you the long, healthy life you deserve. No one can calculate the price you're paying in reduced life expectancy, impaired health and quality of life, but we can easily figure the cost in dollars. When I recently investigated the price of a pack of name brand cigarettes in this area, the lowest price I could find was about $5.00, all taxes included. In many places, you'll pay more than $5.00 for a pack. Depending on how much you smoke, over a single year this could add up to the price of quite a nice vacation. Over several years, this could add up to the price of a college education! Take a look at this table, which is based on the $5 price:

If you smoke this much ...	In ONE YEAR you *burn up* these dollars
One Pack a Day	$1880.25
Pack and a Half	$2737.50
Two Packs a Day	$3650.00
Two and a Half	$4562.50

Did I say "nice vacation"? For the price of a pack and half a day, you could take a cruise to Glacier Bay and Alaska. Two packs a day would just about pay for a week in London or Paris. And remember, those are *after tax dollars*, so the real cost is even higher. Talk about having money to burn!

Will Insurance Pay for Hypnosis for Smoking Cessation?
Almost certainly not, alas. Insurance companies do not like to pay for hypnosis sessions for any reason, despite strong indications that this could save them a great deal of money in the long run.

Can You Take a Medical Tax Deduction?
I am a hypnotist, not an accountant, and obviously I cannot give you tax advice. The following quote from IRS Publication 502 for 2006 was recently brought to my attention, and perhaps you'll find it informative:

"Stop-Smoking Programs

You can include in medical expenses amounts you pay for a program to stop smoking. However, you cannot include in medical expenses amounts you pay for drugs that do not require a prescription, such as nicotine gum or patches, that are designed to help stop smoking."

Again, I cannot give you tax advice, and you should check the current year's IRS publications for yourself.

After You've Quit, Can You Ever Have "Just One"?
It is vital for you to know that with the help of hypnosis you can become totally free of tobacco. However, tobacco contains powerful chemicals. What this means is that if you stop smoking with the help of hypnosis, or by any other means, and then stay free for a year, or ten years, or thirty years, and for some reason decide to have just one smoke, or just one chew, you could find yourself hooked again. It's almost like being an alcoholic, you can't have *one.*

Are there Other Ways to Quit besides Hypnosis?
Certainly there are. Nicotine patches and chewing gums, other programs and even going "cold turkey" all work for some people some of the time. The best hypnosis programs work for almost everyone all the time provided they have really decided to quit.

Hypnotism Programs for Smoking Cessation:

Hypnosis Tapes and CDs
This is the cheapest hypnotic option. It is difficult to get reliable figures on how successful hypnotic tapes and CDs are in turning smokers into non-smokers, but certainly they work for some people some of the time.

What about Group Hypnosis Sessions?

This option is intermediate in cost, and in success rate. Again, reliable figures are hard to come by, but more than 50% of the smokers who attend group sessions conducted by reputable hypnotists succeed in becoming non-smokers. If you have the opportunity to attend a group session, perhaps you should consider it.

One-on-One Hypnosis Sessions

These tend to be the most effective for several reasons. For one, the rapport between the hypnotist and the client is better. In a typical group session, the hypnotist is on stage or behind a podium, and you are one of a crowd sitting in a hotel ballroom.

Typically, when you come to see a Certified Hypnotist for smoking cessation, you'll probably sit next to each other in a comfortable office. As you relax in a recliner, the hypnotist listens to your very own reasons why you became a smoker in the first place, why you continue to smoke, and why you want to stop. He or she will give you personalized suggestions to guide you to freedom from the smoking habit. Depending on the program used by the particular hypnotist you choose, one or more sessions may be required, and they may last from one to two hours,

Another important reason why one-on-one hypnosis sessions are so effective is the commitment you make. You are devoting your precious time to the session or sessions, more than you would for the typical group session or a tape or CD. And the fee, perhaps comparable to the cost of a few cartons of cigarettes, is still more than you would pay for a group session, and you really want to get your money's worth.

I should mention one more reason why you might choose one-on-one hypnosis for smoking cessation. Put very simply, in this writer's opinion it's the best approach. And don't you deserve the best?

How Effective are One-on-One Smoking Programs?

Would you believe 100% effective? By golly, I hope not! Any practitioner who claims 100% success should be looked at *very* carefully. Not all programs are the same -- I can only speak from my own experience, although other hypnosis practitioners using other programs have told me of similar results.

Like any habit, smoking is learned behavior and can be overcome by learning new behaviors. After one intensive session of hypnosis, you are a non-smoker when you leave my office. Depending on your individual needs, this session will last about two hours, sometimes a little longer, sometimes a little less.

Are there any guarantees? As you are well aware, human behavior can *never* be guaranteed. I *cannot* guarantee that every single person who takes my smoking cessation program will become a life-long non-smoker. However, if you were to relapse into smoking within the next few days after leaving my office, a follow-up session would be free.

When working with clients who know that they need to stop smoking but haven't stopped yet because it can be a hard habit to break without some help, I have had *no* requests for a free follow-up session. Most of the people who come to me for smoking cessation sessions are in this category, and succeed in becoming non-smokers after a single two-hour session.

Occasionally I see a client who is conflicted about smoking – a part of her wants to stop but another part of her wants to continue to smoke for some reason – a reason that usually is not obvious. People may offer reasons that are something like these, which I have heard . . .

"My mother is always bugging me to stop smoking. I'll do it when I want to, and not because she wants me too."

"My Uncle Julius smoked until he was 90, and he never got lung cancer - what's the hurry?"

But these are seldom the actual reasons people continue to smoke. In both of these cases, the client started smoking as a form of rebellion against convention or authority, and they still associated smoking with personal freedom and independence. Which is indeed ironic, since they were far from free or independent - they were shackled to and dependent on their cigarettes . . .

With such a client, success depends upon discovering the real reason that they are still smoking, and then getting all parts of him or her to agree that, though that reason may have been important once, that was in the past and it is unimportant now. This may require one or more additional sessions and may or may not be successful.

I don't know of course, but you may want to ask yourself why *you* haven't stopped smoking yet . . . ?

~~~

About Robert M Dunscomb

Robert M Dunscomb BCH is a hypnotist practicing at Hudson Valley Hypnosis in Poughkeepsie New York. Board Certified by the National Guild of Hypnotists, Robert has been helping clients deal with many of the everyday problems of living since retiring from the corporate world in 2002. He can be reached through his Web site at www.hv-hypnosis.com or by phone at (845) 471-0021

CHAPTER 5

Self-Hypnosis

By Marc Carlin

"Your belief determines your action and your action determines your results,
but first you have to believe."

Mark Victor Hansen

Beginning The Process of Programming Your Mind

This is a simple and direct way that you can begin to program your mind to receive the autosuggestions of your choice. I have broken this process down into 5 easy to follow stages, that allows you to become familiar with the trance experience.

Give yourself time to process each stage, perhaps a couple of days, practicing each stage numerous times each day.

Stage 1

I know these simple but powerful techniques will benefit you in your life, as you integrate them into your lifestyle. It will take a commitment on your part, but I assure you, it is an extremely small amount of your time, and well worth the investment.

So, let's get started.

This first stage is about relieving everyday stress. Depending on how much stress you might be feeling at the moment, you might find all of it dissipates, or most, or some. This is a simple method of relieving stress, and the more you do it the better you'll get at it, and the faster you get the results.

Read the instructions through first, and then practice doing the technique immediately afterward.

You can do this either sitting or standing. If you have a problem with keeping yourself balanced, find a place to sit down, or lean against the wall. Take a deep breath in, and as you breath out, close your eyes shut. With your eyes shut, relax the muscles around your eyes until they are so relaxed that they will not work. If you think this is difficult for you, then just think about relaxing the muscles around your eyes until they are so relaxed that they will not work. As you do this, continue to focus on your nice rhythmic breathing.

Now once you are able to do that (getting the muscles very relaxed around your eyes), hold onto that relaxation for about 60 seconds or so. It is just an estimated time at first, so it might just be around 45 seconds or 75 seconds, that's OK. The more often you practice this technique, the closer this exercise will be to exactly 60 seconds. Now once you have held onto that relaxation for that amount of time, open your eyes and notice how much more relaxed, and in control you are.

When should you do this?

Anytime you want to take a break.

1. Weight Loss: If you are using this for weight loss, you would do this technique anytime you think you want to eat something you know would be better off left on the plate, or on the shelf, or on the menu.

2. Stop Smoking: If you are using this for stopping smoking, you would do this technique anytime you think you want to have a cigarette, or think you are craving a cigarette.

3. Stress Reduction: Before and/or after any stress provoking situation.

Have fun practicing this exercise. Do it as many times as you want to during your day. You cannot over do it, however, be safe in where you choose to practice.

In your next stage, , we'll begin the process of using visualization in a unique, easy and fun way to program your mind thru mental rehearsal. When you practice what it is that you want, your subconscious will go out of it's way to make sure you get it.

Stage 2

"It isn't what you have, or who you are, or where you are, or what you are doing that makes you happy or unhappy. It is what you think about."

Dale Carnegie

If you have been practicing what you learned in Stage 1 for a couple of days, by now, you are feeling more relaxed and more comfortable than you were before. But, and this is important, BUT only if you have been practicing the technique. And I mean practicing the technique regularly.

You see, we learn by trial and error. And you are in the process of learning through experience. And you can't have the experience unless you take action. So if you have been taking action, you have been having the experience and you are learning to relax as an act of will. If you had difficulty being relaxed in the past, you will soon be able to relax with just the thought of wanting that relaxed state, as you practice, practice, practice.

What we rehearse, we become accustomed to doing. And mental rehearsal is just as important, as physical rehearsal. In this second stage you learn how to do mental rehearsal without having to put out much effort.

This technique is to be done before you go to bed at night. It's simple, and easy to do, but like all of my techniques, it is extremely powerful. And here it is:

Each night as you go to sleep you will say to yourself, "every day, in every way, I am better, and better, and better" This is an old phrase used by the famous hypnotist from the early part of the last century. This hypnotist, Emile Coue, traveled around the world educating people on the techniques of autosuggestion. Now here's the powerful part of this process. I want you to bring up a picture in your mind of whatever it is that you want to accomplish. If it is losing weight, bring up an image of yourself doing one particular behavior that will result in you losing weight, such as, eating small amounts of food. If you are looking to stop smoking, bring up an image of yourself taking in deep breaths of fresh air feeling a wonderful sense of control. Make this image as if it was a motion picture, and see this image in your mind's eye as you

repeat that phrase ten times to yourself. "Every day in every way, I'm better, and better, and better. And then go off to sleep for the night.

Now since your subconscious mind does not sleep, you have just programmed your mind to do mental rehearsal all night long. This is a great way to do mental rehearsal with minimal effort.

In Stage 3 you'll learn how to go into the hypnotic trance state on command. You'll also learn the secret to creating powerful suggestions to make your subconscious do what it is you want it to do.

Stage 3

"Do not wait; the time will never be 'just right.' Start where you stand, and work with whatever tools you may have at your command, and better tools will be found as you go along."

Napoleon Hill

Before we get to Stage 3 let's review what you have learned and practiced so far.

In Stage 1 you learned a really simple technique on how to get relaxed as an act of will. You are no longer at the mercy of the things going on outside of you. You can be concerned, and be able to respond in a satisfactory way, but you do not have to stress out about it. Because you now have a tool to de-stress.

In Stage 2 you learned a way to do mental rehearsal without putting out much effort. By using the power of your subconscious, while you are sleeping you have practiced the behaviors and responses that you want to become your conditioned responses.

Ok, now we're onto the process of teaching you how to go into hypnosis on command, and how to give yourself suggestions for change.

1) Continue doing Stage 1, the relaxation on command when necessary and Stage 2, the Pre-Sleep Technique you already learned.

2) In addition, do the following:

Sit in a comfortable chair with your back and head supported.

Focus your eyes easily on a spot opposite you, slightly above your eye level, about 45 degrees up. It could be a spot on the wall high up, or the corner of a picture frame, etc.

Take 3 deep breaths. Hold your third breath for the mental count of 3, and as you let it go with a sigh, close your eyes and feel your whole body relaxing even more.

Just RELAAAAX and allow yourself to go into a deep hypnotic rest.

As you relax in your seat, feeling relaxed, feel your breathing begin to become regular and slower than it was before. Now imagine yourself on the top of a staircase with 10 steps.

As you walk down each step, slowly, think to yourself the words " deeper and deeper". Use your imagination and really start to feel yourself going down the stairs and continue to think to yourself," Deeper and deeper."

By reaching the bottom step, you've become so very relaxed and calm, you will be in your hypnotic state for today. Remain in this state for as long as you can and still remain comfortable. Make it about 5-10 minutes to start. Allow your mind to go wherever it goes.

3) When you are ready to emerge from trance, count forward from 1-5 With each count imagine yourself more vibrant and energized than before. Think to yourself, "I feel better mentally, physically, and emotionally, than before."

By practicing this technique, you are making it easier and easier for you to access this level of relaxation. Your mind and body are practicing relaxing in unison. And this ability to go into this very relaxed state, both mentally and physically, becomes easier and quicker for you to achieve.

In Stage 4, I'll show you how to give yourself the suggestions that will re-program your subconscious mind for success.

Stage 4

"Not to have control over the senses is like sailing in a rudderless ship, bound to break to pieces on coming in contact with the very first rock."

Mohandas Karamchand Gandhi

I trust you have been becoming better at guiding yourself into trance, relaxing as an act of will, and allowing yourself to accept the positive suggestions for the changes you are looking to make.

This is Stage 4 of this 5 stage process of learning Self-Hypnosis.

In Stage 1, you learned a really simple technique on how to get relaxed as an act of will. You are no longer at the mercy of the things going on outside of you. You can be concerned, and be able to respond in a satisfactory way, but you do not have to stress out about it. Because you now have a tool to de-stress.

In Stage 2, you learned a way to do mental rehearsal without putting out much effort. By using the power of your subconscious, while you are sleeping, you have practiced the behaviors and responses that you want to become your conditioned responses.

In Stage 3, you learned how to guide yourself into a deeply relaxed state. This is the first level of hypnosis. The first level of hypnosis is enough to begin behavior pattern changes through autosuggestion.

Ok, now we're onto the process of teaching you how to go into hypnosis on command, and how to give yourself suggestions for change.

The more you practice self-hypnosis, the better you will become at it. You will soon realize that you can achieve not only a deeper level of relaxation but you will be able to achieve it faster.

Giving yourself Autosuggestion:

1) Figure out what it is that you are looking to accomplish. Is it a change of habit? behavior? thought? Whatever it is, have a clear image of what the outcome will be like. This can be what it is that you will look like, what your behavior will be like, what you will feel like, etc. You can use that image, or if you have trouble holding onto the image, you can connect a key word to

that image that represents that image to you. This will be your prepared thoughts that you will use when you reach your level of self-hypnosis.

2) Get yourself deeply relaxed to the first level of hypnosis (See Stage 3).

3) Once you reach the last step and feel completely relaxed, test your eye closure. Tell yourself in your mind that you can not open your eyes, they are shut tight. After you test them and can not open them, stop and continue to relax.

4) Now, you are ready to give yourself autosuggestions. The autosuggestion will be the image or keyword(s) you have previously chosen. See your image or keyword(s) over and over, vividly in your mind's eye.

For each new goal, do this exercise at least 21 days in a row then continue for reinforcement. Be patient and you WILL achieve your results.

Stage 5

Now basically, you've gotten the techniques down to affect powerful change from the inside out. This stage will give you examples of how to formulate suggestions for the most common complaints people see me for.

Now that you have gotten even better at going into trance, reducing stress, and relaxing on cue, we are going to teach you the fundamentals of creating suggestions for change.

In Stage 1 you learned a really simple technique on how to get relaxed as an act of will. You are no longer at the mercy of the things going on outside of you. You can be concerned, and be able to respond in a satisfactory way, but you do not have to stress out about it. Because you now have a tool to de-stress

In Stage 2 you learned a way to do mental rehearsal without putting out much effort. By using the power of your subconscious, while you are sleeping, you have practiced the behaviors and responses that you want to become your conditioned responses.

In Stage 3 you learned how to guide yourself into a deeply relaxed state. This is the first level of hypnosis. The first level of hypnosis is enough to begin behavior pattern changes through autosuggestion

In Stage 4 you learned how to go into hypnosis on command, and how to give yourself suggestions for change.

Now, in this 5th Stage, I'm going to show you how to formulate suggestions before going into trance so you can program your mind to achieve that goal.

"Suggestion" is how you specify what your goals are and then give your subconscious specific instructions to get those goals. This puts your conscious and subconscious minds on the same page. And once that happens, you are almost guaranteed success.

When formulating suggestions for self-hypnosis, you want to be specific about what you want as an outcome. You might have heard the expression: Be careful of what you wish for. I think this came about because of this focus on only outcomes instead of what the desired effect is. For example: if you give yourself a suggestion for attracting lots of money and don't make it very specific, this might be a problem. You can get money as a result of some kind of insurance windfall because of a tragedy. This would probably not be what you want.

If you were wanting to lose weight, and that was all that you focused on, that could lead to you losing weight through harmful ways, which would most assuredly not be what you want. (In the movie "The Devil Wears Prada, I remember one of the main characters saying excitedly, "I'm just one stomach virus away from goal weight!" – I thought that was funny, but not a desirable thing to program yourself for!)

So be specific in the formulation of your suggestions. Also add a benefit that you will get when you follow the suggestion.

And as promised, here are some suggestions you can give yourself for weight loss:

"I enjoy eating healthy food and my body feels good when I do"

"I eat slowly and get to taste my food fully"

"The healthiest foods taste the best to me"

"I exercise daily and feel invigorated when I do"

"When I exercise daily, I get a sense of accomplishment and confidence that stays with me all day"

When you give yourself these suggestions, bring up an image of you behaving as the suggestion suggests.

Auto suggestions for Smoking Cessation would be as follows:

"I am a non-smoker and I have more time to do the things I want to do"

"I am a non-smoker and my lungs feel better breathing fresh clean air"

"I am a non-smoker and I feel calmer and more in control"

"I am a non-smoker and my clothes smell fresh, my hands smell fresh, my hair smells fresh, my mouth smells fresh"

"I am a non-smoker and people accept me more easily"

"I am a non-smoker and I breathe more easily and I am more calm"

~~~

About Marc Carlin, The NYC Hypnotist:

Marc Carlin is a noted author of numerous articles on hypnotherapy and NLP that pertain to enhancing performance and reaching ones true potential. He is a practicing hypnotherapist, sports pro, teacher and coach for more than 25 years. He has his own private practice on Long Island, New York, as well as Manhattan, New York, where he is responsible for helping individuals reach their full potential.

Further information about Marc's services can be found online at http://www.hypnoticstate.com.

CHAPTER 6

HYPNOTRITION:
Thoughts as Food, Foods for Thought
for Body, Mind, and Spirit
by Deborah Yaffee

"Change your menu, change your life!"

Whether you call it the body-mind or the mind-body connection, your own experience tells you that what goes into your mind affects your body and what goes into your body affects your mind. Of course, there are numerous scientific studies that demonstrate exactly what parts of the brain are involved and how this all works, but the simple truth is that our thoughts are food and foods fuel our thoughts.

There are many ways to achieve and maintain optimal health, but I have enjoyed phenomenal success for myself and my clients by distilling these ways down into a simple formula that you can apply to the sacred trinity of your being: Body, Mind and Spirit. It is the Life Balancing Formula of Cleanse, Replenish and Tonify.

Mind: Thoughts As Food

HypnoCleanse:

Did I mention that some people call hypnosis "brain washing" as if that were a BAD thing? What hypnotists actually do is help people change their minds...in a good way. The truth of the matter is that we are in the DE-PROGRAMMING business! It's our job, pleasure and privilege to help <u>you</u> cleanse your mind from the caked on sludge of self-limiting and erroneous beliefs that have been keeping you from manifesting the positive intentions for your life.

How many of you have "<u>wanted</u> to lose weight" or are "<u>trying</u> to lose weight"? And one week into your diet, you go to that party at a friend's house and there's a BIG piece of chocolate cake with the ooey gooey icing on it and, oh my gosh, it has YOUR name on it! At first you bring out your willpower to remind yourself that you are not eating big pieces of cake anymore.....but that darn piece of chocolate cake bursts into a siren song that you just can't resist and ..... oops, oh well, tomorrow is another day, and as long as you messed up with the cake , you may as well make a day of it and have the fried chicken, the chips, the dip, the bread, and that high octane punch, right? How did this happen??? Did the devil make you do it? Of course not... it was the devil's food cake that made you do it. Hmmmmm........

Or are you one of the thousands of people who watched The Secret, got all fired up and spent days and days affirming that you ARE a millionaire...and then found yourself in even greater debt on the credit card for that purchase of the Next Best Home Business Opportunity. What happened?

What happened was that you didn't clear out your closets and clean up the house before opening the door to a lifestyle that your subconscious mind considers a very unwanted guest. Your conscious mind may recognize and decide that those extra 35 pounds have put your health and wellbeing at risk, and it is your conscious mind that recognizes and decides that you would like to be financially free. But the conscious mind is only the 10% tip of your beautiful mental iceberg….the other 90% of your mind is operating below the surface. We call it the subconscious mind (SCM).

Most of the database files in the SCM are organized by association. Think of the word "red" and watch how many general and personalized associations arise when you think, picture, or imagine "red". Once a file has been accepted into the subconscious database, similar information is stored there, too. For example, you may have learned very early on that whenever you screamed from hunger as a baby, someone came and fed you. As time went on, your caregivers may have given you food EVERY time you screamed, whether they knew if you were really hungry or not. What they observed was that you DID stop screaming, usually, when someone stuck some food in your mouth. Years later, as an adult, you consciously may understand that you are not hungry and not needing to eat, but your dear old SCM is feeling downright upset about something and is screaming for the only pacifier it has ever known: food! It is holding to an association between food and comfort that has a very long, reinforced history. If you really want to change your food habits and release the unhealthy pounds, you are going to have to bring the SCM onto the same page as your conscious mind.

As we bump into life, we may unexpectedly, and unconsciously, dislodge some of these old associations. If our mental closets are packed full with old toys, tattered ideas and beliefs that are too small for our grownup lives, the door will open and all the clutter will come spilling out….and we'll have one awful, unwanted mess to clean up. When our mental database is cluttered and filled with outdated files and programs that are full of bugs, we need to purge the system…clean out those closets so that we can get ourselves a new wardrobe of beliefs that are a perfect fit for the person we have become --- and for that person we are "if only….".

In order to put something new and different into our lives, we need to first make a space. We need to cleanse and de-clutter our minds from all those things that are holding us back from stepping into our greatness. In my experience, hypnosis, Emotional Freedom Technique (EFT) and Zpoint Process have been the most useful tools for cleansing the mind of those pesky limiting beliefs. Each of these modalities is especially designed to uncover and clear erroneous beliefs and self-defeating habits from the SCM. Experienced practitioners of these arts will guide you to liberate yourself from the prisons of your own experience and making. I'm sure you will now agree that a little "brain washing" can do a Body-Mind good!

Want a deeper, more immediate mental cleanse? Then get rid of your ANTs as well! ANTs are Automatic Negative Thoughts. ANTs can be annoying or downright destructive, but they don't have to be difficult to get rid of. All it takes is the Raid Formula of vigilance and clearing. With a little practice, you can become so accurate when you aim that spray of vigilance, that you can hose down and clear an ANT in an instant. Stop feeding your ANTs and enjoy your picnic!

HypnoReplenish:

As we empty the old limiting beliefs and self defeating habits from our minds, we can begin to replenish and renew them with positive thoughts, images, and feelings.

We need to use replenishing language. Words are powerful. Language changes the way we set our intention; it transforms us from "wanting to lose weight" to "releasing unwanted pounds of fat." Adjusting your language can change your results from "trying to eat better" to "choosing the healthy choice in every moment".

Our minds create images from words, and images are the first language of the SCM. The SCM responds to images with feelings. Feelings lead to action….and it is the actions we take that build our lives, for better or worse. Therefore, the words and images you give yourself, and the feelings you induce in your being are of the utmost importance for replenishing your mind after you've cleansed away unwanted beliefs and habits.

Replenishing the mind is FUN! First determine what you WANT and then imagineer your way back to the future a few minutes every day with self hypnosis. The SCM only knows the present moment, so affirm the future of your desire as if it were already here. How do you FEEL? What do you SEE? Does your new life have a SMELL? What do you HEAR? WHO is there? HOW do they look?

Action follows thought, so put in writing what you WANT. Use affirmations to flex the appropriate subconscious mental muscles by focusing on what you want rather than strengthening the "what you don't want" muscles. Charge your affirmations with "the attractor factor" by infusing them with the magnetic energy of big excitement. Putting them in writing reinforces the message you are sending and quickens their manifestation. From the comfort and confidence of your REALITY, upgrade your affirmation to the status of decree by proclaiming powerful "I AM" statements.

HypnoTonify:

Like your muscles, the mind needs to be kept exercised and toned for optimal functioning. We want the mind to be alert, strong, quick to respond, adaptable, limber, balanced.

Here are 4 easy ways you can begin today to tonify your mind:

1) One especially effective way to keep your mind resilient to stress is to keep it saturated with positive words and images. Make a list of words and images that inspire and uplift you, words and images that express how you would like to feel. Choose one or more and allow your mind to dwell gently on them. Notice how your whole being relaxes and finds equipoise in the peaceful refuge that words can conjure up.

Joy…Tranquil…Softness…Puppy…Heart…Wonder…Innocence…

2) Location! Location! Location! I once heard that "environment is stronger than willpower". Whether it's your internal environment of positive thought, or an external environment of the type of positive, energetic, happy, kind, and loving people that make you feel good, put yourself in positive environments. Reduce the time you spend with IMPs (Interminably Morose People). Build up your reservoir of tranquil equanimity by being with positive people in positive environments. If you can't find one, create one!

3) Practice your ability to freely choose your responses to life. Choice can be conscious or unconscious. You can train your SCM to choose wisely and quickly by taking the time to train it now with conscious effort. Humans get better with practice so start with small choices and work your way up to more important ones. When life gives you lemons, make a martini with a twist.

4) Be mindful of your self-talk. Your body-mind (SCM) hears every word you say ...and takes it seriously, so be careful what you ask for because your dutiful SCM is very likely to manifest it for you. Be kind and tell yourself good things about yourself. Praise your strengths and accomplishments. Give yourself a nicer future by reminding yourself that you are doing better and better every day, in every way. Ask your hypnosis professional to give you some good post hypnotic suggestions to sound a corrective alarm to any negative declarations that are part of your habitual self conversation.

Body: Foods for Thought

It sometimes happens that a hypnosis client has successfully cleared the past issues that contributed to their excess weight, and they have replaced destructive behavior patterns with positive behaviors of healthy eating and exercise....and yet they are not experiencing significant weight release. What's going on?

Well, as renowned weight loss hypnotist, Tom Nicoli, likes to say, "Hypnosis is magical but it's not magic." Sometimes it's not just mind over matter. Sometimes it's bad biochemistry resulting from trying to satisfy the body's nutritional requirements with a national food supply that is nutritionally bankrupt and the physiological stress of toxic substances in our air, food, and water.

When we give the body all the essential nutrients it needs to be the miracle that it is, the body comes naturally into homeostatic balance: hormonal systems calm down, excess fat is released, mental focus increases, the skin glows, and vexing cravings for excessive salt, sweeteners, sedatives and stimulants vanish without effort.

Nutritional Cleansing:

Over the last 30 years, research from many prestigious universities, health organizations, and even the U.S. Environmental Protection Agency has demonstrated that it is not a question of IF the environment and beings on this planet are carrying around toxins, but HOW MANY and how those toxins are impacting the health of the planet and its inhabitants.

It's no secret that our world has become hazardous to our health. Heavy metals, petrochemicals, herbicides, insecticides, chemical fertilizers, noxious hydrocarbons, food additives, genetically altered materials, antibiotics, synthetic drugs, and hormones are among the substances in our water, earth, air and food that have created a life-negating broth in which our cells are simmering on a daily basis.

So who needs to cleanse? In a word: Everyone.

There are many types of physical cleanses and I am sure you have heard of some of them. You may have even tried one or two. Many cleanses are either harsh purgation protocols that target one particular system of elimination, like the liver or colon or kidneys, or they are starvation fasts. In addition to nutritional protocols, purified water, good fresh air, and getting the body into movement on a daily basis are integral parts of any cleansing program.

The type of cleansing that I use and share with others is a gentle system of advanced nutritional cleansing for the whole body. In advanced nutritional cleansing, we give the digestive mechanisms of the body a rest while simultaneously feeding it a concentration of nutrients and special components to draw impurities out of the cells throughout the whole body.

Nutritional Replenishing:

Although organically grown whole foods are better for you than loading up on junk food, it has been known since 1936 that modern farming practices in the U.S. were depleting the soils to such an extent that the nation's health was clearly declining. Even where savvy farmers have made the effort to re-mineralize their soils with rock-dust, acid rains destroy the organisms that transform the minerals into the organic forms that our hungry cells can absorb and utilize. So, after cleansing, we want to flood the body with high quality total nutrition that will support a well-balanced blood and brain chemistry and that will help to build our immune systems, healthy cells and healthy cell membranes. Such a mixture will also support and enhance the important detoxification pathways in the liver.

For this, the body needs a full complement of amino acids, vitamins, minerals, essential fats, enzymes, probiotics, fiber, and organic soil acids. Modern advancements in food technology have made pure, total nutrition available in ways to use that are easy and inexpensive. Whole, un-denatured organic whey protein can be combined with a special blend of natural sugars, enzymes, probiotics, vitamins and minerals in absorbable forms to make super food shakes and is, in my opinion, an ideal food for replenishing our depleted bodies.

Many people who are sensitive to commercial dairy products are able to tolerate pure, un-denatured whey protein remarkably well.

Tonifying the Body:

Tonics are herbs, foods, and other nutrients, like certain vitamins and minerals, that may have a certain amount of detoxifying effect in the body but their most striking property is their ability to restore balance in the body by their ability to exert their activity in either direction. For example, ginseng is a tonic herb that contains some ingredients that lower blood pressure and some that increase blood pressure. The wisdom of the body discerns which group of ingredients it needs when the tonic is consumed. Whatever is not needed at the time is eliminated or metabolized. Ginseng belongs to a category of herbs called adaptogens. They work in a gentle manner to help the body adapt to internal or external stresses by signaling the appropriate physiological systems to do more or to do less to meet the needs of the circumstances. Adaptogens are fantastically useful for cross-correcting the body for sleep issues, energy issues, strength and stamina, and immune system issues.

Since ancient times, Eastern medical practitioners recognized the need for tonification on a daily basis. This is something far more sophisticated and complex than just balancing the acid-base ratio of the blood. Tonics help the body be more resilient to both internally and externally generated stress. They increase the body's adapt-ability by strengthening the nervous system, the immune system, and the glandular systems. In doing so, they increase our resistance to disease and the adverse effects of trauma. Our 21st century lifestyles expose us to incredible amounts of stressors 24 hours a day, 7 days a week. We need tonifying!

A good tonic formulation includes an ample supply of anti-stress, body-balancing herbs, minerals, enzymes and other substances to revitalize and rejuvenate the body.

Conclusion: What's on YOUR Menu?

I hope I have helped you appreciate that nutrients are physical "suggestions" we give our bodies, and that words, images, affirmations and hypnotic suggestions are nutrients that feed the mind.

The waltzing heartbeat of a balanced life is sustained by a regular rhythm of Cleansing, Replenishing, and Tonfiying. Cleansing begins with awareness and acknowledgement of what needs to be released or cleansed, and simply accepting it as it is. We then apply methods of cleansing that are safe, appropriate and efficient. After cleansing, we Replenish ourselves with all things positive and continue to keep our new life well-oiled and polished by Tonifying on a daily basis.

If you've been on a steady diet of mental, physical and spiritual junk food, you need to cleanse, replenish and tonify. Techniques like Zpoint Process (www.yourzpoint.com) and the spiritually-based practice of 7th Path Self Hypnosis™ (www.riversidehealing.com/7thpath.htm) are elegant methods to help you to clear and rejuvenate your mind and spirit. For the body, I have found the 30 day advanced nutritional cleansing program at www.cleanseforsuccess.com to be the easiest, gentlest, and most effective for producing rapid and lasting results.

In every moment, you can make a healthy choice. I invite you to change your menu and change your life!

~~~

About Deborah Yaffee:

Deborah Yaffee, CH, CN is a Nutritionist, Forgiveness Coach and a Certified Hypnotherapist in good standing with the National Guild of Hypnotists. She integrates nutrition, hypnosis, energy psychology, Reiki, prayer and meditation into her consulting practice. She is an experienced nutritional cleanse coach and enjoys serving clients worldwide via telephone sessions and email support.

Would you like to learn about <u>Hypnotrition for the Spirit</u> and more about Automatic Negative Thoughts (ANTs), especially the most dangerous varieties? Ask for the complete version of this article and your free information package about how I can help speed your personal transformation with Hypnotrition, email deb@riversidehealing.com

CHAPTER 7

Self Hypnosis

by Garrett G. Buttel

"There is nothing supernatural or magical about hypnotism, and there is not one documented case of harm coming to anyone as a result of its therapeutic use. Although its benefits are well established, it remains a misunderstood and often-dreaded subject in the minds of the general public. This resistance stems from our natural fear of any powerful force we do not understand. Ironically, there is a much greater danger in not understanding it. This force does not come from the Hypnotist, but from your own subconscious mind, and if you do not control it, it controls you. Most of our physical ailments and mental depressions are the result of this uncontrolled power working against us when we could easily be using it to our advantage".

CHARLES TEBBETTS

ARE THERE THINGS IN YOUR LIFE YOU'D LIKE TO CHANGE?

Many of us go through life wanting to change — we even think that someday we will. However, in the back of our minds, we also think it will result in another failure, or it will be too hard, or we'll do it some other day. We wander through life continually justifying why we're staying the same.

There is a better way and there is more control right at your fingertips. Many people make all kinds of changes easily and assuredly. The way is hypnosis, and better yet, we can do it all by ourselves with self-hypnosis. Self-hypnosis is exactly what the name implies; it is with you and only you, no one else is involved. We all have noticed how our mind often seems to contradict itself at times. For instance, maybe we need to change, we tell ourselves that from now on we're going to act a certain way. However, when the time comes we can't change because there is anther part of our mind that wants to keep things the same. The conscious part constantly is analyzing – thinking. Often it thinks too much and causes people problems like insomnia. This constant thinking can be thought of as the noise of our mind and when we can quiet the noise, then we can contact the part that gives us the automatic reactions – our subconscious.

Why spend time to learn self-hypnosis? Simply put, *the rewards are stupendous.* You can take control of your life and will be amazed at how many different ways self-hypnosis can help you. A great hypnotist, Dave Elman, understood all about hypnosis and used self-hypnosis on a daily basis. His son wrote that one Sunday they were taking a drive and Dave had to empty his bladder so bad that he didn't think he could make it to their next stop. Dave was in a jam, but from the back of the car came three words, "Use self-hypnosis Dad!" Even a person who used self-hypnosis every day didn't think of using it in that position, but it worked!

What can you use self-hypnosis for? There are hundreds of uses. For one, it gives you the ability to take a five or ten minute power nap any time you need it and come out feeling refreshed and ready to go for hours. I also show many of my clients just how easy it is to have anesthesia with hypnosis. It is a better anesthesia then the chemical kind and much less toxic. Some other uses for self-hypnosis are setting goals and keeping them, getting ahead in your profession, weight and addiction control, and conquering your fears. Many successful people have used it for enhancing their creativity and have enabled their subconscious to supply previously unthought-of answers. With mental imaging and positive suggestion people even have overcome chronic diseases. *There are over four hundred different ways that hypnosis can be used to make your life happier and more fulfilling.*

HOW HARD IS SELF-HYPNOSIS TO LEARN?

Learning self-hypnosis is easy. I know, I taught it to myself quickly and used it to lose over one hundred pounds before I even went to a hypnosis class. After I took a few courses on hypnosis, I learned different ways to do self-hypnosis and unfortunately got confused. I thought there were more effective deeper states and searched for more powerful methods to get into them. Not so. My ignorance of the state set me back for awhile. Finally, I realized that I had learned to quickly get into the state by myself. Just like other natural states of mind, for example daydreaming — it doesn't matter how you get there, when you're there you're there.

Later in the chapter, you'll read about my easy way to do self-hypnosis, but first I want to briefly explain what hypnosis is. In our divided mind we have one part that analyses, thinks, and rationalizes. This is called the conscious part. We also have another part that reacts automatically without logical thinking. This part helps us survive by learning and doing what is needed to safely exist. This automatic, reactionary part is called the subconscious. Our subconscious is programmed similar to a computer with instinctual programs and many other programs that start from the time we are born. These programs are for our protection, our survival, and there is even a guard that ensures they stay unchanged. Often, even if a program happens to be there in error and is working to our disadvantage, it is guarded. As long as what is being done is perceived by the subconscious to keep us alive, the subconscious is happy to continue, and resists change. Throughout our formative years we learn thousands of things that are done automatically. Our subconscious is programmed with the information that keeps us alive. If we have a painful experience, we quickly learn not to do that.

Again, the subconscious is an automatic reactionary mechanism that has no logical abilities. Once it gets the program it is very resistant to change because these things are for our pleasure and survival. This is why we sometimes have programs going that are not good for us. For example, our subconscious may pick up the idea that eating helps to distract from distressful emotions. This causes a person to subconsciously go for something to eat rather than experience the distressful emotion. The subconscious is doing its job – going from pain to pleasure. However, the pain that's on the other side of overeating is not understood by the subconscious.

Replacing an erroneous program with a new healthy program is what self-hypnosis does. Often there just is no other way to change and this is why people who use self-hypnosis, in general, have a more successful and happier life. Once you learn self-hypnosis your self confidence zooms. You realize that you can change – and it's easy. It's liberating. It's exciting. There is nothing scary about hypnosis. It is neither magical nor mystical. It is a normal state of mind that we are constantly in and out of in our daily lives. It is the best and often the only way to change.

HOW TO DO SELF-HYPNOSIS

Before I went to hypnosis classes, from self-study, I understood that in order for our mind to relax, we initially had to relax our body. First get into a very comfortable position (one that you are sure not to fall out of when you relax every muscle). Lying in bed or on the floor, sitting in an arm chair or against the wall — these types of positions allow you to relax completely. Take a nice deep breath and as you exhale say to yourself in a confident tone, *RELAXING*

NOW. Do this three times and imagine each time that every muscle is going completely relaxed from the top of your head down to your toes.

I picked up on the odd necessity to then take my attention to my eyelids and relax them completely. Do that next. Once you know your eyelids are completely relaxed, test them to make sure they don't work. You know that if you tense the muscles your eyelids will pop open, but that's not the exercise. Keep those muscles relaxed and then attempt to open your eyes without tensing them. You will find that your eyebrows may move but your eyes will stay shut. Test them until you satisfy yourself that they aren't working and then imagine another wave of relaxation from the top of your head down to your toes and let every muscle go as relaxed as your eyelids. You will now feel profoundly relaxed. You know you could move an arm or leg if you wanted to, but you just don't feel like it.

The next step is to relax your mind, and this I did by imagining I was in a *no-thinking chamber.* This chamber was very comfortable and no thinking was allowed. I was amazed at how long I could go without a thought and often would catch my mind thinking, "Wow, I haven't had a thought for a minute or so." Then I would realize that *that was a thought* and I had to let it go. I let it go by watching it rise in the chamber in a balloon and disappear above (using your imagination is fine because imagination is the language of your subconscious). I then went longer without a thought — each time longer. Very shortly I found myself in a little dream and then coming out of it, just like we do before we fall asleep at night. I call this state the see-saw state, and you'll find that you can stay in this enjoyable see-saw state as long as you want to. It doesn't take long, a few minutes of no thought and your mind automatically goes into this state. Practice this for a week many times each day.

If you find you are having trouble in the no-thinking chamber do this deeper. Start counting, in your mind, from two hundred backwards and between each number say, "R e l a x i n g   n o w". Say it as if you are ordering your mind to relax. Continue, 199, R e l a x i n g   n o w … 198, R e l a x i n g   n o w … etc., until you notice you forgot where you were. It shouldn't take long — then switch the exercise to saying the word *"one"* over and over to yourself as if you're saying a mantra in meditation. Continue until you notice that you had a little dream and are coming back.* You are there. Stop, relax further, and let your mind ride the see-saw.

If by chance after practicing this for two weeks you still can't get it, then I suggest going to a hypnotist or getting my six CD set that will much more gradually teach you the skill.

HOW TO GIVE YOURSELF POWERFUL SUGGESTIONS

Once you're able to get into the see-saw state needed for self-hypnosis, you are ready to learn how to use it to make powerful changes in your life. Basically you need to give your subconscious the correct ideas; however the twist is that the subconscious doesn't think in words, it thinks in pictures. You need to paint a picture with your words of exactly the way you will be after the change has been made. For example, if you are having difficulty going to sleep, the first thing to do is choose the positive motivating desire, which of course is to get a good night's sleep and feel refreshed in the morning.

Sit down and write a paragraph about it, painting the picture something like this:

Because I want to get a full night's sleep and feel refreshed each morning, each night when I go to bed, I relax every muscle in my body and enjoy the feeling. I know I can easily fall asleep because I always did before. After a few minutes I am so relaxed that I easily drift into a deep restful slumber that continues all night. If for some reason I need to awaken, I am able

---

* Self Hypnosis and Other Mind-Expanding Techniques, Charles Tebbetts, 1987, Westwood Publishing Company Inc., pg. 43.

to return to bed and go back to sleep within seconds. I enjoy relaxing in bed and find my mind easily shuts off any thoughts until the next day. I sleep soundly and comfortably and awake feeling wonderful — completely rested. All of these thoughts come to me in hypnosis, when I think of the code word "SLUMBER."

(see below for use of code word)

Basically the paragraph should follow these guidelines.

THE MOTIVATING DESIRE MUST BE STRONG – focus in on one change or even part of it. As you become successful your confidence grows and you can venture on to other things.

BE POSITIVE - for example do not say, "I will not eat between meals" but rather say, "My meal fills me up so much I can easily go from one meal to another feeling satisfied."

ALWAYS USE THE PRESENT TENSE – your change is happening now, not in some vague future.

SUGGEST ACTION NOT THE ABILITY TO ACT - Don't say, "I have the ability to speak well" but rather "I speak well, in a pleasant assertive tone.

BE SPECIFIC - Choose a self-improvement suggestion you are anxious to carry out and work with that one suggestion until it is accepted. Don't suggest a number of things at once.

USE REPETITION – In both the number of times you restate the paragraph (if recorded) and in the number of times you do self-hypnosis.

Now that you have the paragraph there are a few ways to get your subconscious to accept the ideas. One is to record the paragraph and play it back when you are doing self-hypnosis. You would need to leave a blank space in the beginning to allow for time to get into the state. When recording the paragraph you have the opportunity to rewrite it again in other words and make the suggestion longer.[*]

Another way to give yourself the suggestion is to have your paragraph with you when you are ready to do self-hypnosis. Read it to yourself three times with the code word. Then go into the state and allow your mind to imagine the pictures of your paragraph. Each time you come back from a little dream you say to yourself only the code word and then relax deeper.

EMERGING FROM SELF-HYPNOSIS

Emerging is not any harder than coming out of a good daydream. You are always in control and can emerge anytime you wish, however time slips by so fast during such an enjoyable state that you may want to set an alarm clock. Better yet, you can use your mind as a clock. Try it, you will be amazed. All you need do is first say to yourself, "I am going into self-hypnosis for two or five or ten or whatever minutes." I find that looking at a digital clock and visualizing the time it will be when you want to finish is helpful. Then go into the state and see what time your mind awakens you. You don't need to count or even think about the time, your mind will very quickly learn to be exactly on time.

There is nothing to be afraid of when doing self-hypnosis. You are always in control. Sometimes in the beginning our skin cells get so relaxed it seems like they need to be scratched. Very quickly we become accustomed to this and it goes away. If this happens it is actually a good thing because you know then that you are where you want to be or very close to it. If you need to scratch, for instance, and your subconscious has accepted the idea that you are so relaxed

---

[*] Note: the code word is not needed for recorded suggestions.

that you can't move your arm, then just give yourself another suggestion, "I can move my arm and when I put it back I'll go even deeper." You are the boss – you are your own hypnotist!

IMPORTANT: Don't forget to give yourself a final suggestion before opening your eyes. Something like this, "On three I'm going to open my eyes and I'll feel great, 1,2,3 open." You'll be surprised at how good you do feel. Also, every time you wake up from sleep you are naturally in this state and have an opportunity to give yourself powerful suggestions. Before you open your eyes every morning give yourself a great suggestion to start your day.

In conclusion, remember that this is the way I taught myself to get into the mental state necessary for powerful self-hypnosis. I was very successful with it and that probably was because I was very motivated. I hope you are as successful. If not, don't give up. Having the power to use self-hypnosis is a precious addition to your life and it's worth whatever is necessary to learn. There are many books about self-hypnosis, but the easiest way to learn is to have a few sessions with a hypnotist. Self-hypnosis with good well informed suggestions will certainly help you to have a happy and healthy life.

~~~

About Garrett G. Buttel

Garrett G. Buttel is a board certified hypnotist with the National Guild of Hypnotists. He is also a member of the International Medical and Dental Hypnotherapy Association. Garrett holds a graduate degree in counseling and worked many years for the Veterans Administration in this capacity. When he realized the great potential hypnosis has for helping people, he attended courses with The Omni Hypnosis Center, The Banyan Hypnosis Center, and The New Jersey Institute of Hypnosis. He has been a Consulting Hypnotist for eight years and retains an office in Belford, New Jersey. Garrett also authored a book entitled, <u>Solving The Smoking Puzzle</u>.

His web sites are: www.MonmouthHypnosisCenter.com &
<u>www.SolvingTheSmokingPuzzle.com</u>.

CHAPTER 8

Winning The Mental Game:
Using Sports Hypnosis to Play Your Best,
All The Time

By Tobin Slaven

"Ninety percent of the game is mental;
The other half is physical"

- Yogi Berra

Amateur and professional athletes around the World are in a constant search for the newest technology in training and equipment, lured by the drive for competitive advantage. It is no surprise then that the most accomplished in every sport are finding impressive results by developing their game with preparation in the area of mental skills training. As hall of fame basketball coach John Wooden and professional golfer Bobby Jones both remarked about their respective sports, "the game is played between the ears, every bit as much as between the lines."

It is the beauty and drama of sports, that a game, season, or career can turn on a single spectacular moment, when inches and split seconds make the difference between champions, legends and those who "also ran."

Sports hypnosis has become one of the most proven methods for extracting peak and consistent performance for athletes seeking to raise their game to the next level. As many competitors know all too well, the best-conditioned body will only perform as well as the mind will allow.

When athletes and coaches ask us, "Why try hypnosis?" – our HypnoGym answer is "Can you afford NOT to utilize hypnosis as a way to maximize your performance for peak and consistent results, when your competition is seeking the same kind of advantage?"

Benefits of sports hypnosis training include:

Heightened concentration and laser-like focus

Overcome self-defeating scripts and release mental blocks, slumps, or fears

On command anxiety reduction for relaxed alertness

Identification and development of triggering mechanisms for the "Zone of Optimal Activity" or (ZOA)

Motor memory adoption of model skills and abilities demonstrated by premier athletes

Integration of training objectives, motivation, and locus on control

Shorter and better-managed recovery periods for fatigue and injury with techniques of rejuvenation and revitalization.

Sports are an ideal laboratory for testing human potential. Hypnotic techniques and mental skills training are literally, like watching psychology in action. With the aid of statistics, athletes and coaches are able to measure improvements with each and every contest. With its seasonal drama and high emotional content, nothing captures our imaginations more than witnessing the triumph of the underdog team or athletes who perform beyond expectations. Hypnosis itself provides the means to debug the brain from problematic behaviors, and program our subconscious mind for confidence and a success mindset. The end result is for the athlete to be able to play their best game, and do it with consistency.

Sports Hypnosis techniques and interventions may be organized into the following five categories for enhanced athletic performance. These categories are considered the essential tools of a comprehensive mental skills training program.

1. Testing, Preparation and Targeting

While it might appear overly simple, a successful mental skills training program will "begin with the end in mind," by creating a clear and concise picture of the desired results each given athlete is striving to reach. Using Neuro Linguistic Programming's (NLP) Meta Model interview structure enables the sports hypnotist to illicit key information about an athlete's current mental strategies – both those that are working well, and those may need to be cleared away or altered.

In addition, client and practitioner can jointly establish clear metrics that will measure areas of improvement, providing feedback that is both informative and motivating.

In some cases testing procedures might also be utilized to rule out physiological limitations that would prevent athletes from accomplishing their stated objectives. Preliminary testing insures preparations that will later avoid the destructive consequences of asking an athlete undertake tasks for which they are not physically capable.

A second critical function of the testing phase is to determine each given athlete's "Zone of Optimal Activity" or ZOA. Athletes perform their best with a certain amount of tension or anxiety prior to and during competition. In fact, many athletes feed off the energy of the moment to post their peak performances. Pre-game butterflies become a signal or fuel for certain competitors. Research indicates that too dampen or disengage this process could potentially have negative effects, so each individual's ZOA is established early thru the Meta Model interview.

Hypnotic age regression is a second technique that may be employed to gather information in defining one's ZOA based on prior experience. Once the zone has been established, anchors installed in the later categories can be used to reproduce the ZOA on command. Other hypnotic techniques such as autosuggestion and post-hypnotic suggestion may be used for this purpose as well.

This is one area where sports hypnosis differs greatly from other hypnotic and even traditional coaching interventions. Conventional therapeutic approaches often attempt to depress the competitive mindset so critical to motivation for top athletes, by creating acceptance and comfort in failure. A more productive approach would engage the benefits of competitive motivation to augment an athlete's game preparation.

2. Counter-conditioning for Anxiety

One of the most commonly recognized benefits of sports hypnosis is the ability to use hypnotic techniques to manage the extreme stress levels that often accompany high-level athletics. Months and sometimes years will be dedicated to prepare for the "Big Game." Many athletes will naturally or thru years of coaching reinforcement, employ coping mechanisms such as superstition or pre-game routines as a way to circumvent anxiety-producing situations.

Utilizing the individual information gathered in the Testing, Preparation and Targeting phase, a successful sports hypnotist will identify the needed ZOA for an athlete and build anchoring techniques specific to their needs. This is the key to a successful specialization in sports hypnosis, as research has indicated over-relaxing some competitors can hamper their optimal state for performance.

Hypnotic techniques to counter-condition against anxiety producing situations will meet two key criteria: 1) the ability to trigger the relaxation response in a rapid fashion; 2) the ability to temporarily suspend the overly reactive mind, which is known as the primary source of anxiety and loss of concentration.

When pre-game anxiety becomes an issue for competitors, physical symptoms may include feelings of physical weakness, muscular tension or tightness, and a general susceptibility to fatigue.

Readers may recognize this as the fight or flight syndrome, where adrenalin is dripped into the body by the sympathetic nervous system. This state of mind is marked by initially preparing the body for trauma or an emergency situation. For an athlete entering a contest however, this natural reaction may leave the body drained of energy, greatly impacting endurance athletes. As fatigue increases, athletes will begin to experience the slight loss of muscle motor memory so critical to the skill sports, where technique determines the best from the rest.

Sports hypnosis techniques are designed to provide the mental and physical boost that accompanies a clear and focused mind. Athletes can approach their moment in a cool, calm, and confidant manner by getting "in the zone" and on command. This confidant mindset then becomes the platform form which athletes can view stress-producing situations from a more productive perspective – an opportunity to thrive on the available challenges and adversity.

3. Mental Rehearsal – The Holodeck of the Mind

Mental rehearsal is an age-old technique enabling practitioners in all fields to use their imagination to "practice" accomplishing their objective prior to engaging with reality. Research indicates that the magic of mental rehearsal lies in the mind's ability to equate real or imagined events, for equal benefit. This provides nearly unlimited opportunity for an athlete to mentally project their participation in every imaginable circumstance, and at varying levels of challenge.

Calling upon a reference from Star Trek, athletes can utilize the "holodeck" of the mind to enter the competitive space and make as many repetitions as needed, all without exposure to fatigue or injury that sometimes results from over-training.

The Olympics are a prime example of athletes employing mental rehearsal because of the years of training required for ultimately results in a relatively short period of competition. Many times have we seen on television a skier silently preparing for their downhill run, swaying and bobbing as they mentally follow the course to the bottom of the mountain. Recent studies indicate that as much as 90% of U.S. and Canadian Olympic athletes have integrated mental skills training into their practice regiments.

Other examples of mental rehearsal techniques include reframing for an internal locus of control, and time distortion. One example of such changes in perception during competitive play would be fast time/slow time manipulation, where basketball legend Larry Bird would describe how he felt like he was playing the game at a different speed than his opponents. Hockey great Wayne Gretzky described a similar phenomenon where his awareness changed to the point where he did not see the opposing defenders, but rather the space between them leading to an opportunity for a shot on goal. In both cases, Bird and Gretzky were not known for their physical prowess, but for their abilities to seize the opportunity and make plays in pressured situations. It is very likely that the top athletes in every sport are using similar techniques thru the means of naturally occurring hypnosis. Day dreaming a buzzer beating shot is an example of a naturally occurring mental rehearsal. In fact, wouldn't you put your faith in the athlete who has hit that shot a thousand times in her imagination before ever walking out on the court?

4. Elimination of Distracting and Inhibiting Psychological Factors

Another major area of hypnotic intervention in sports is the elimination of self-defeating scripts and mental blocks that can develop in an athlete's psyche. Athletes are not always aware or able to recognize the internal talk that fuels subconscious programming. Thought stopping and substitution techniques are often taught to neutralize negative self talk habits.

Hypnoanalysis can be used as a research tool to discover mechanisms underlying physical performance. In the case of one professional baseball player, a mid-season slump was reversed after hypnosis was used to reveal specific corrections in his swing – corrections to which the player was not consciously aware prior to hypnosis.

In a second example, a professional golfer made major improvements in his game after working with a sports hypnotist. The hypnotist aided the golfer by installing suggestions that he would be oblivious to environmental stressors, such as people in the gallery. By hypnotic suggestion, the golfer was increasingly able to envision a dotted line between the ball and the cup, often times seeing his target two to three times larger than average. As his confidence and game developed, he also received suggestions that he would not be shaken by a bad shot, but would retain his internal locus of control. Additional suggestions centered on employing the practice of seeing every stroke in success before beginning his swing. As stated earlier, this pre-visioning of the desired performance is essential for top achievement in any field.

Imagine for example, a gymnast who suffers a fall or injury while performing a back flip. The way our mind functions, that "failure" may be forgotten, or it may begin to run like a negative program that is reinforced every time he or she imagines delivering their floor routine. Fearing a repeat mistake or being hurt, the athletes may then begin to pull out and not complete the maneuver, creating a block for themselves. Just as easily however, mental rehearsal can used to program desired results – in fact one could argue that that is the only way anything in this world is accomplished. It is said that no event comes to pass, that was not first a thought flashed across the movie screen of the imagination.

5. Training to the Point of Failure – Blowing Away The Comfort Zone

The fifth and final category of techniques rests on the coaching maxim of development by pushing an athlete beyond their comfort zone. It is human nature to maintain the physical and psychological security of known experience. Seeking to grow the area of one's athletic comfort zone, we introduce the concept of distress and eustress to manage the development cycle. Distress is the anxiety-ridden state described in category #2 while eustress provides the butterflies, the excitement, and the mental edge that competitive athletes use to their advantage.

When an athlete's skill development slows or training becomes stale, it is often an indication that they are staying in the circle of comfort most of the time. Since all positive changes and growth take place outside of the comfort zone, change is painful. This is the reason why many athletes reach a peak in their skills and abilities; they become unwilling to put up with the growing pains of change.

Sports hypnosis is useful in bridging this gap, both physically, mentally, and emotionally. Many times athletes will recognize the need to push the envelope physically, because a little bit of pain equals faster, stronger, and more flexible. An athlete recognizes at least physically, the benefits far outweigh the discomfort. Using age regression and progression techniques, a sports hypnotist can help an athlete create the optimum learning environment – essentially giving the athlete a chance to test the waters at a manageable pace.

The outer edge of the comfort zone can only be expanded by training to the point of failure – which can be a daunting task for many athletes. Hypnosis provides the ideal environment to experience the awkward and uncomfortable phases that often accompany learning, without over shocking the system.

Summary

There are a myriad of ways that hypnosis can be used to augment and program performance and skill acquisition for athletes. We have established five categories that also provide a protocol for introducing hypnosis in the competitive arena.

It is clear that sports hypnosis can differ from conventional coaching or even hypnotherapeutic techniques that might be unwittingly employed without awareness of the competitive mindset. This chapter provides a brief summary for the athlete, coach, or hypnotist seeking to enable peak performance in a safe and reliable manner consistent with the spirit of athletics.

If you would like to learn more about the use of hypnosis in sports, I encourage coaches and athletes to browse some of the available research that is available online, In particular, case studies relevant to their chosen sport might prove useful in demonstrating how other athletes have benefited from similar training. Ultimately, the best information will come with direct experience and sports provide the ideal learning laboratory. Prior competition and training results provide the baseline to which sports hypnosis and mental training programs can be measured for improvement.

More specific information on fast and easy techniques that meet the standards cited above will be available in *The MVP MindSet: The Mental Skills Training Handbook for Coaches and Players Planning to Win the Mental Game*. By this same author (available Fall 2008).

~~~

About Tobin Slaven:

Former high school and collegiate athletic coach Tobin Slaven M.Ed. is a National Guild Certified Hypnotist and founder of HypnoGym™ Hypnosis Center. With over 10+ seasons coaching team sports and doing group seminars, Slaven explains that the results are clear: "The mental edge is what separates the good from the great, demonstrated time and time again, at every level of competition - in athletics, and the Game of Life. Whether you want to remove obstacles, tap into your potential, or develop mental toughness – hypnosis training is the key to unlocking the door."

To learn more about HypnoGym and our proven system of cutting edge technology in how to *'Train Your Brain for Health, Wealth, and High Performance,"* visit www.HypnoGym.com.

ABOUT THE EDITOR

The Editor, Steve Roh, is founder of Center City Hypnosis in Philadelphia. Through the use of advanced, intensive mind-altering techniques, he's helped hundreds of people "clean house" mentally and emotionally. If you're a motivated individual looking for greater focus and confidence so that you can take action and reach new levels of success, visit www.CenterCityHypnosis.com to learn more about gaining the hypnotic advantage.

In addition to being featured on cable television news and radio programs as an expert on hypnosis, Steve is a contributing author to "The Ultimate Success Secret" by Dan Kennedy, one of the world's leading direct marketers and copywriters.

For more information:

Contact Steve at info@centercityhypnosis.com

Voicemail: 267-303-0036

Fax: 866-224-7559